HeadGames

Defeat the competitors in your head!

HeadGames
Defeat the competitors in your head!

Joanne Love

Illustrations
by
Pasquale Di Iorio

Joanne Love
2016

Copyright © 2016 by Joanne Love

All rights reserved. This book or any portion thereof may not be reproduced or used in any manner whatsoever without the express written permission of the publisher except for the use of brief quotations in a book review or scholarly journal.

First Printing: 2016

ISBN 978-0-9944058-3-8

Joanne Love
Melbourne, Australia
www.joannelove.com

Dedication

To all my family...

It's a privilege to share my business, life, and love with you. Thank you for all the help!

Contents

Acknowledgements 9
Introduction 11
PART ONE 13
The Scoop 15
PART TWO 29
Mindset 31
Self-Awareness 35
Optimism 39
Resilience 57
Are you Growing or Fixed? 73
Keeping up with the Kardashians 85
PART THREE 91
Self-Confidence 93
Get Ready 99
Know your Masterplan 103
What's your Mantra? 107
Monkey See, Monkey Do 111
Conquer the What if's 115

Picking up the Pieces	119
Create Success	125
Success Breeds Success	131
Exploit others Success	137
Be an Ego Master	141
Superstition	143
PART FOUR	145
Anxiety	147
Melt Down	149
Focus	157
Get Repetitive	169
The Latest and the Greatest	173
The Finish Line	177
References	179

x

Acknowledgements

To Annette....

Thanks for your terrific editing, the finest chocolates in the world can't do your efforts justice.

To all my other staff...

Thanks for your patience, tolerance, advice and thank you for adding the last little bits to the final version.

Introduction

You're not alone. You may feel like you are alone, especially when the shit hits the fan, and the "other competitors" in your brain start their own game against you. Regardless of whether you are an experienced or a novice athlete, there will always be an occasion when you will feel overwhelmed or defenseless to those thoughts.

I know, what a cruel and cold world the inside of my head can be...and I'm only a coach. I can only imagine what is going on in yours!

It's okay, help is on its way. This book will teach you how to control those "other competitors" in your head and defeat them once and for all. Let's get started! Let's learn how to focus on being your best, and to make each performance count!

PART ONE

The Scoop

The Scoop

> *"Nothing can stop the man with the right mental attitude from achieving his goal; nothing on earth can help the man with the wrong mental attitude".*
>
> Thomas Jefferson

We really want to perform well, but just before we compete some little voices get started inside our head. You soon start to focus on the things that can possibly go wrong rather than the things that you can do right. Or you start to think what you can't do rather than what you can do. Before you know it your confidence is shot!

Or...
We have all been to that event. Your expectations are high. You have trained hard, and your taper has gone to plan. You are feeling on top of the world, or you were……. until you walk into the competition arena, and then all of a sudden your world comes crashing down. Your anxiety overcomes you and you choke!

There are two major obstacles that get in our way when competing.

- Self-Confidence
- Anxiety

As athletes, we tend to forget that the activities that are taxing on the body can also be taxing on the mind. If your mindset isn't right, then results can be devastating. Let me explain.

Happy and Thriving Competitor Model

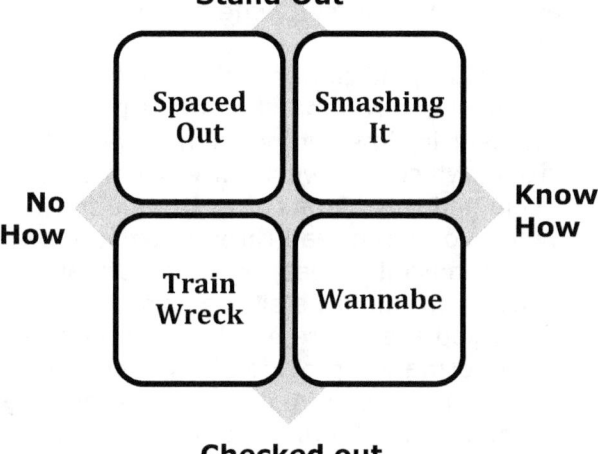

From the model on the previous page, on the horizontal continuum is the psychological knowledge you possess about handling big events. At the very end is "**no how**", in other words you know nothing, whilst at the opposite extreme is **"know how"**, you have the knowledge to make change and keep cool under pressure.

The vertical continuum is all about mindset: going from "**checked out**", at the very bottom, to **"standout"**, the very best mindset you can have, at the top. You might think you have a good mindset, but after reading Part Two, you will be able to assess for yourself whether you do or don't.

Each quadrant of the model represents where you may be at this present moment in time. No position is set in stone, which you will realize when I have explained the **"Smashing it"** quadrant. When you have read through each of the four quadrants types, try and work out where you might be sitting right now. Once you are aware of where you are, the information provided in this book will help you to move up into the **"Smashing it"** quadrant. If you are already there, you may find some of the techniques in this book useful to create future improvements in your performances.

Train Wreck

When you are sitting in this quadrant of the model, you are failing more than you achieving. Personal bests or memorable performances are few and far between.

When your mindset is poor and you have "**no how**" to fix these issues, then it is really easy to become a train wreck, skittling off the rails when you competing. And sadly, yes, you will be failing, and facing decisions, such as, is this all worth it? One of the saddest examples of a train wreck athlete is Sally Robbins or "lay down Sally" as she was later labelled. Not only did she suffer failure personally, but she also inflicted its damage on her fellow rowing team members.

The infamous "Lay Down Sally" incident occurred at the 2004 Athens Olympics. Sally was a member of the Australian women's eight rowing crew. With 500m to go the Australian team was only three seconds behind the Romanian crew who were out in first place. In the final 400 metres Robbins gave up, dropped her oar, which dragged in the water, and laid back on teammate Julia Wilson's lap. Australia, consequently, finished last, ten seconds behind the fifth place crew.

A journalist reported that directly following the event, the hostility from her teammates was insane. The Australian media ridiculed her, and gave her the label of "Lay-down Sally". Even the PM weighed in, saying it wasn't the Australian way to just quit like she did.

But the real tragedy behind the whole story was that this wasn't a first occurrence for Sally. In the women's quad scull at the 2002 World Rowing Championships in Seville, Sally had already performed a similar stunt, costing Australia certain victory. 2000 Olympics silver medalist Rachael Taylor was quoted as saying:

"Australia was blitzing the race, leading the entire field all the way. It was as about as sure a thing as you could get to having the world title in the bag, when with approximately 400 metres to go Sally Robbins stopped rowing. The Australian crew dropped back and finished in fourth position. Sally's three teammates were understandably shocked, devastated and inconsolable: not at all dissimilar to the sickening re-enactment I witnessed on Sunday."

Years later in a NSW supreme court defamation trial, it was actually acknowledged that Sally had quit up to seven times previously in races. Reading through transcripts about the race. It was obvious to all that she lacked the mindset qualities needed to be an elite athlete, such as resilience and a growth mindset.

Whilst I don't personally know Sally, it is her explanation of what occurred in those event, which leads me to believe that the extreme mental pressure of "the big day" event was just too much for her to handle psychologically. What is even sadder, is that no-one took Sally aside and helped her to prepare for the psychological stresses that might tip the balance during this world-class event, especially given her previous issues.

Anxiety is often amplified when the sufferer feels it is taboo to express how they feel. Similarly, anxiety will also surge when there is a feeling of being trapped. So for Sally, confined in a boat with seven other rowers, the odds were against her from the start. In her own words she described what happened as "paralysis", just like a deer caught in a spotlight.

Spaced Out

You may have the best mindset in the world, but without the "know how" you will constantly be on the back foot. Your performances can range from spectacular to woeful; in other words, hit and miss. When everything is going well you have no issues; you love competing, enjoying the atmosphere, and you are producing the results you want. Yet for some reason, when it is important to you, the results just don't eventuate. Everything seems to be surreal, things just don't go to plan and you are left wondering why.

Wannabe

You may have been given the "know how" but because you don't have the right mindset, it really is only hearsay to you, and you never work at applying it correctly. This often results in your efforts on the field falling flat. Later in this book you will hear the story of John, who spent numerous hours in the lead up to the Olympic selection trials with a psychologist. Unfortunately, it was his mindset which ultimately let him down. His fixed mindset affected his ability to create the adjustments needed, and as he never really absorbed what he was being taught, he couldn't apply it when he needed it. For example, whilst he was spoon fed what he needed to do for one event, he couldn't apply that instruction to do it for any others, because he had a "I know it" already mindset. In fact, Carol Dweck in her book Mindset, says that those with a fixed mindset mainly try to hide any deficiencies, even if it puts their future success at risk.

Smashing It

Throwing tantrums to smashing it, is exactly what Roger Federer did. As a sixteen-year-old it was not unusual for Federer to throw his racket in disgust at failing to win points. He was regularly kicked out of practice sessions because of his bad behaviour.

At seventeen, he made the decision to change. He worked with a psychologist to improve both his mindset and to learn all he could about dealing with pressure situations, to ensure that the talent he held didn't go to waste. A prominent psychologist Roland Carlstedt, upon hearing that he was doing this work, stated, that his future rivals didn't stand a chance. How true that comment turned out to be.

> *"Roger's just got it all – when you have the technical, physical and athletic foundation that he has, that's probably three-quarters of the battle. Add to that the immense confidence that brings, along with the very strong athlete's [psychological] profile that I think he*

fits, and he's virtually unbeatable."

So imagine what you could do if you could improve your mind by even ten percent. What would ten percent difference look like?

I've been working hard on some strategies to help you overcome the competitors in your head and hopefully you can put these to use for good and not evil. Firstly, you will learn all about what mindset you need to be a great athlete….tally ho…

PART TWO

Mindset

Mindset

For success it is essential that you have a good mindset. This is really step one, because without a good mindset, you fail to learn what is offered and you are resistant to change. Your mind is a wonderful tool, and even scientists are only starting to grasp its magical abilities.

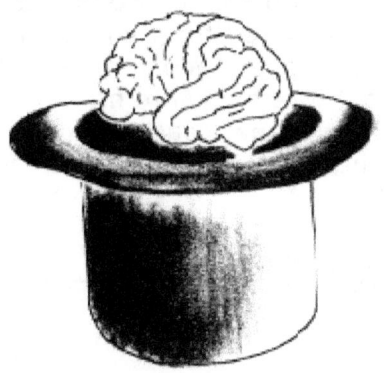

You mind is just like a computer that can be programmed, to run games. You choose which software is installed; is it productive or unproductive? You want to play a game on your computer, is your software making it run fast enough or is it slowing it down? Like your computer where you have control over the software, you also have control over your mindset. For example, how you tackle things in your head is reflected in your actions.

For some younger athletes, our software was programmed into our brains at a very tender age by people such as our parents or teachers. This impacts and affects your behaviour today. The good news is, just like a computer we can remove this software for a better version quiet easily. All that is required from you is the effort to make it happen, and some self-awareness about where you are now.

Did you know coaches find it really easy to help athletes who have the right mindset?

Coaches love it when you are:
- Being grateful that someone cares enough about you to push you to improve beyond where you would get on your own.
- Being honest and open enough to know you're not perfect.

- Being able to handle critical feedback (even if it hurts).
- Working to actively change bad habits.

Whilst coaches find athletes are not coachable when:
- They take feedback as a personal affront.
- They seem ungrateful
- They read more into things than they should.
- Training and competing is all about you, and you get very upset when someone else interferes with some aspect of your day.

There is a very quick and easy mindset quiz on my website.

(http://www.joannelove.com/mindset_quiz).

Go on take the test, if you score anything less than 50, you still have some work to do. Before we learn anymore about developing a great mindset, let's start with building self-awareness.

Self-Awareness

Over the years, we have all watched contestant auditions on shows such as 'X-Factor'. There are many potential 'stars' who screech out a song, only to be laughed at by the judges. Often, those that 'bomb' are surprised that the judges could even think they were bad.

Why would they put themselves out there on national television to be ridiculed by all? Sure, some are in it for attention or to have a joke, but for others, who truly believe they can be the next 'Australian Idol', they fall into the category of lacking self-awareness.

Over the years, I couldn't tell you how many times I have heard coaches ask athletes things such as "can't you feel that", or "how does that feel", only to have athletes respond, "No" or "I don't know".

Becoming self-aware about your mindset is much the same, as knowing where you are now, and allowing yourself to be open about change will stand you in good stead, with sport and also life.

Building self-awareness in your mindset is relatively easy when you know how.

Start with comparison

Whilst normally, I would tell you not to compare yourself to anyone, it can be a great way to see people with great mindsets, and compare your attitudes to theirs in certain situations. Take the great Michael Jordan, a fantastic example of an athlete with a great mindset.

Think about how you compare to Michael Jordan, in the way you react to challenges, failures, or opportunities for taking risk. Michael Jordan was actually cut from his high school basketball team, but he didn't let this deter him. Instead of giving up, he doubled his practice time each day, and finally made the team.

What do you do when you fail?

Learn from the best athletes in your sport. Compare these attitudes to see where you stand.
1. How often do you complain or bristle when someone suggests you are wrong?
2. Are you a good loser or a bad loser?

3. How often do you blame others when things go sour?
4. Do you take tough feedback well or switch off?

Awareness is the beginning of creating mindset change. Don't stop at just the comparison, but also take note of the triggers that cause you to project that poor mindset. When you are prepared for those triggers, you will then have greater control over your mindset, keeping it in check for better outcomes.

Now we have created awareness about our present mindset let's begin learning about the features of a good mindset.

Optimism

There are some people who subscribe to the theory that we are all born to be optimistic, and it is the world we live in that makes us pessimistic. Think about the media and the news they deliver to us every day; we are consistently fed bad news. Why?

Because out of all the pieces of information we receive every day, the media has learnt that this type of news is the one we seek the most. We are more receptive to anything drastic. The human brain evolved in a hunter-gatherer environment when immediate action was needed to survive. Studies continue to show that our brains are hardwired to respond to negative events more than positive events. It is little surprise, with all this bombardment, that we become more pessimistic and that life seems so much harder than before.

One researcher, author, and prominent authority on optimism, Dr. Martin Seligman, believes that children are extremely optimistic until they reach puberty. Think about you at ten years of age, remember how excited you were each practice session. What about now?

Now, you are probably that athlete who is nowhere near as optimistic in their outlook, as you once were?

Are you:
- stressed out by your workload, i.e. trying to balance sport and study.
- driven by that elusive time goal or place, and therefore trying to deal with all the inherent stresses it brings.

So the more successful you become the more the pressure of competition serves up problems. Unfortunately, what happens to many athletes, when edging towards being elite, they lose sight of the journey, lose sight of who they are and how they got there. They lose appreciation for the value of people who don't win, and have a tendency to lose their optimistic outlook on the sport.

What can you do to change this outlook? It's very simple and all will be revealed shortly. I have included this topic early, because being optimistic will help you improve in many other areas, as well as bring back that FUN element to your training and competing.

What is Optimism?

> *"Optimism is faith that leads to achievement. Nothing can be done without hope or confidence. ... No pessimist ever discovered the secret of the stars, or sailed to unchartered land, or opened a new doorway for the human spirt".* - Helen Keller

An optimist is someone who sees the silver lining in every cloud and views the world through rose-tinted spectacles.

Being optimistic has been shown to have wide ranging benefits from everyday well-being to improved health outcome and success in all areas of life.

A study conducted in the late 1990's, on new law students, found that optimism helped prevent sickness during times of stress. Ninety first-semester law students were tested to find whether they were optimistic or pessimistic by nature. Then scientists looked at the amount of T-Cells and natural killer cells, which fight infection and disease, they had in their bodies. Eight weeks later, this same group of students were retested, and it was found that the optimistic students had more T-Cells and natural killer cell activity, whilst the pessimistic students' protective cell counts decreased.

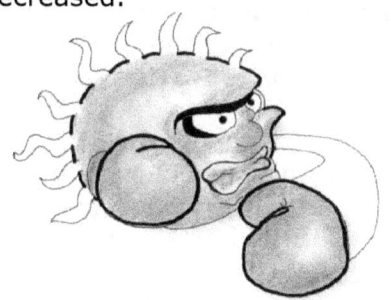

Similar studies have confirmed that optimists have "fewer illnesses and doctor visits...and longer survival times"[1].

Carver and Scheier (2002) claimed that optimists are less likely to abuse drugs and alcohol, whilst pessimists are more likely give up on things[2].

Optimists accept the reality of the situation

Pessimist deny or avoid the problems

Optimists try to put the problem into the best possible view and confront it head on, whilst pessimists have a tendency to escape the problem by drinking, sleeping, or eating[1].

How is optimism helpful to you? Below is small list of some of the many studies that show optimism aids athletic performances.

- Footballers who were more optimistic had better performance and less variability with those performances[3].
- Athletes who were more optimistic overcame adversities and had greater motivation and persistence[4].
- Higher-rated optimistic basketball and baseball teams had more wins[5].

- Optimistic swimmers performed with less variability[6].
- Optimistic athletes showed less tendency to burn out[7].
- Athletes who are optimistic will be more persistent in the drive towards a goal and can tolerate hard work[8].

One brilliant example is that of the great swimmer Matt Biondi, winner of 8 Olympic Gold Medals. Biondi was part of an optimism study undertaken in the early 80's by the psychologist Dr. Martin Seligman. During training, Biondi and his teammates were timed under race conditions, and then told that their actual results were slower than what they really achieved. The swimmers then repeated the event, and Biondi swam faster than he did the first time. This was in contrast to those teammates who were labelled as "pessimists." In fact, one swimmer, who was classified as a pessimist, "sat and rocked like a baby in a corner for twenty minutes afterwards"[6].

Biondi lives by his motto:

"Enjoy the journey, enjoy every moment, and quit worrying about winning and losing."

Biondi was the obvious favourite for the 100m Butterfly at the 1988 Seoul Olympics. He had won every 100m Butterfly race for the last two seasons.

The media and the American public were relying on this to be a US win. Little did anyone expect that he would lose by 0.1 of a second to a relatively unknown swimmer, Anthony Nesty, from Surinam. After coming third in the 200m Freestyle earlier in the meet, then following up with only a silver in the 100m Butterfly, many in the media were starting to write him off.

They considered his meet was over, and he could never return from such poor performances. However, Dr. Seligman didn't write him off; in fact, he was confident he would bounce back. Biondi did just that, going on to win Gold in his next five events at the 1988 Olympics, and making him one of America's most decorated athletes.

Seligman's theory is the best for understanding and helping to build your optimism, so an explanation of it follows below.

Seligman's Learned Helplessness

Helplessness occurs when we believe we have no control over our environment. A significant link has been found between how we think about causes of events, and our levels of optimism. Seligman gave the label "explanatory style" to explain how we attribute our success and failures. In fact, in many of his learned helplessness studies, those who exhibited pessimistic traits, "learned" to give up. Nothing they did mattered, SO WHY TRY?! Some suggested reasons why athletes become pessimistic include, losses, and highly critical parents – yet optimists also experience these issues. The difference between the optimists and pessimists is how they respond to these adversities. Optimists always assume that things will get better, whilst pessimists opt to believe that things will always be hard or difficult.

Explanatory Style

Understanding the explanation, you give about your sporting performance is important. This style will influence your future performances and development, and if left to be pessimistic in nature, it could be detrimental to any future success.

The three dimensions of the explanatory style: Permanence, Pervasiveness, Personal: are summarized below with examples of each.

PERMANENCE - Results are considered in terms of permanency. Are good or bad results due to permanent causes, or temporary ones?

OPTIMIST has a **TEMPORARY FOCUS** "The next race will be different."	**PESSIMIST** has a **PERMANENT FOCUS** "I never win anything"

PERVASIVENESS - Is the failure or success confined to a specific event, or is it all-encompassing to you personally?

OPTIMIST has a **UNIVERSAL FOCUS** "Kicking in the rain was hard, I think everyone suffered."	**PESSIMIST** has a **SPECIFIC FOCUS** "I am no good at kicking a football."

PERSONAL - Who is responsible for the failure or success? Internal (self) or external (others) causes?

OPTIMIST has an **EXTERNAL FOCUS** "We weren't ready for that team today; they played so well."	**PESSIMIST** has an **INTERNAL FOCUS** "It's my fault, I didn't play well enough; that is why we lost."

By now you are probably wondering if pessimists can become optimists. The collective answer from many years of research is YES. People are constantly changing and can be optimistic at some points in their lives and not at others. Optimism can be learned, both unconsciously by observing people around us, or explicitly, as with other skills.

There are two notable ways to initiate change:
1. Isolating stressful beliefs, then challenging and changing those beliefs.
2. Take every opportunity to problem solve, make goals, and set decisions to improve.

What does this mean for YOU?

We have a natural tendency to respond to events with a particular explanatory style. That is, you form habits that dictate how you will respond to future events in your life, whether it be positive or negative. Changing this is as easy as learning the ABCs, or in this case, ABCDE.

Alter your pessimistic path by following this simple process.

A = Adversity

Identify the adversity, meaning the objective description of what happened, not your interpretation of it. For example, was it just a bad performance, or were you expecting to win?

B = Belief

Belief focuses on how you interpret the adversity. Negative beliefs usually cause a distortion of the truth. Focus on the positive alternatives instead. You hold a negative belief when you continually focus on not winning when you're expected to, even though you did a massive Personal Best (PB). Focus on the PB because you can't control winning the race.

C = Consequences

Consequences amount to your feelings and what you do in relation to those feelings. You need to learn to separate thoughts from feelings. For example, if you feel sad, then you are sad. When you have had what you consider a bad performance, what are your feelings and what did you do when you felt those feelings?

Often when you are upset your feelings can be rather extreme, (just ask your mother), fortunately the facts are not. So, if you are saying something like: "I'm a loser, everyone is better!" you need to understand that this really means "It feels like everyone is better than you – at the moment"

D = Distraction and Disputation
Ask someone close to you like your coach, another athlete or family members to distract you with these simple thought-stopping techniques. For example, get them saying "blah, blah, blah" when you start mouthing off with something negative.

SOCIAL

Or, in the training environment, it can be something as startling as blowing a whistle. For competition day, place a rubber band on your wrist, snap it every time a negative though prevails. Or, distract your attention elsewhere, such as, concentrating on a handheld game.

With disputation, you need a note book to analyze the facts. Be a detective, look at the evidence. Is there any? In the case of expecting to win, it was just that, an expectation, there is no real evidence suggesting that you would win. You can't control anyone else's performances.

Another example, "you never do well in races", it's time to get out your magnifying glass and be a Sherlock Holmes. Analyze what you can change, and what can be done in the future to increase the likelihood of success.

Have these questions at the ready:

- Were you over-confident?
- Were you ready to race?
- What critical mistakes did you make with your performance?

It is important for athletes to learn from their mistakes. It can help to ask another team member or your coach for their views on your performance. Just remember to pick the right person who can give the right critique. If the negative belief is correct, for example, you really didn't perform well, ask "what are the implications?"

In other words, is the world going to end? Are you going to die? No, it's just a race.

Lastly, sometimes we all have a tendency to hold onto useless consequences. For example, you may have a belief that life isn't fair, but that sort of thinking doesn't do anything for anyone. In this case, look to the future. "Is the situation changeable? How can I go about changing it?"

E = Energization

I particularly like this last part. Energization done well, helps tremendously when things don't go to plan. When this happens think about your favourite player, what would they do in this situation, and then narrate a story. Start with identifying your athlete, ideally one already at the top, and "ask" (imagine) what they would say after a tough performance. Imagine or research how they have dealt with their own challenges. Every sport has examples of winners who also lose, this is the norm.

Now you have achieved some optimism in your sport, and hopefully your life as well, you are ready to learn about resilience.

Resilience

When you have resilience, you have the ability to overcome adversity, bounce back from failure or trouble, respond positively to pressure and challenges, and then adapt to move forward towards greater success.

Whilst we know that optimism is important for success, we also know that resilience is what allows athletes to keep coming back when the odds are against them.

In fact, the man who started the optimism push, Martin Seligman (whom we discussed in the last chapter), now promotes resilience.

You can test this yourself. Seligman created the positive psychology unit at Penn State University in America. If you google Penn State University optimism, you will find no links, but if you google Penn State University resilience, the first link is all about their Resilience program. In fact, their Resilience program is now more important than their Optimism or Positive psychology program.

Resilience is important!

Athletes must be able to cope with pressure, both from internal and external sources.

They need to stay motivated when things don't go as planned. They need to know how to set goals which they may not achieve, and be able to learn from them and move on.

INNATE FACTORS

Lastly, they need to able to compete and train when things aren't going 100% for them. Maybe they are not feeling well, or they are dealing with some family issue. Unfortunately, bad things happen to all of us. We've all witnessed a football game where a player has gone on to play a really great game, even though his family has suffered a tragedy in the days leading up to the game. That's resilience!

The good news is that resilience can be taught. Being resilient means that you will respond better after a failure, bouncing back and hopefully, increasing your likelihood for success in the future.

Just for the record, here is a list of successful people who didn't let failure get in the way:

Bill Gates: Gates dropped out of Harvard and starting a business with Microsoft co-founder Paul Allen called Traf-O-Data. This earlier idea didn't work, but Microsoft sure did!

Walt Disney: A newspaper editor sacked him because "he lacked imagination and had no good ideas". I am sure every child (and adult for that matter) would thank that newspaper editor a million times over after visiting Disneyland!

Albert Einstein: History tells us that Einstein did not speak until he was four and had trouble reading, causing his teachers and parents to think he could be mentally handicapped. He was expelled from school and was refused admittance to the Zurich Polytechnic School. While he might have been a bit slow at the start, he went on to win the Nobel Prize and change modern physics theory.

Elvis Presley: Luckily for us, Elvis didn't stop performing when he was fired after his first performance and told to "go back to drivin' a truck."

And lastly, one of the greatest athletes of all-time:

Michael Jordan: Jordan believed failure was part of success:

> *"I have missed more than 9,000 shots in my career. I have lost almost 300 games. On 26 occasions I have been entrusted to take the game winning shot, and I missed. I have failed over and over and over again in my life. And that is why I succeed."*

Firstly, what makes some spring back from failure whilst others crack with pressure? There are so many Olympic Silver Medallists who have lost a race by less than one hundredth of a second, but they get back up and try again and again.

Resilient people have been found to be more flexible and can adapt to new situations both quickly and easily. In fact, they usually flourish in challenging situations. They happily acknowledge that they can bounce back from adversity, and their confidence ensures that they will. Instead of seeing failure as bad luck, they see it as good luck, or the road to more successful outcomes in the future.

One of Australia's greatest distance swimmers, Kieren Perkins, is a true testament to being resilient. At the 1996 Atlanta Olympics, Kieran struggled into Lane 8 of the 1500m final. In his own words, he stated, "I wasn't ready. I wasn't good enough".

For those who don't know, Lane 8 is given to the slowest qualifier. Just four years earlier Kieren had won the Olympic Gold medal in this event and was considered to be the hot favourite. For swimmers in this position, self-belief plays a huge part, and there would have been some part of him wondering whether he could actually produce a winning result or if perhaps winning was beyond him.

In Australian Story (ABC, 2014), Kieren shared what he remembered was going through his mind just prior to the start of the final, "Are you going to let all this fear and uncertainty and doubt cloud you and worry you into doing a bad performance because you've lost your mind and you're not able to deliver?

"It was so simple, but so obvious, and I mean the weight of it all just lifted. I was a different person in a moment". When

Kieran failed to land Lane 4, the fastest lane in the final, commentators and fans were all behind the "other" Australian, Dan Kowalski, to bring home the Gold. The race started, and Kieran took the lead. In fact, he held the lead from the start to finish.

Even Kowalski acknowledged later that he didn't have the mental toughness that Kieren possessed, and not being able to see him over in Lane 8 didn't help his chances. When Kieren finished his race and he knew he was the gold medal winner, he leapt out of the pool and ran to gratefully acknowledge his future wife for her support through this arduous journey, "We did it. We did!" he proclaimed.

Things weren't the same for Dan Kowalski. Dan says he "cried myself to sleep for almost 18 months just because the dream was over".

Some of the traits that Kieren displayed in this race are those that have been found to boost resilience which are:

Self-Belief	The extent to which you have confidence in your ability to address problems and obstacles that you encounter.
Optimism	You always have a positive outlook on events.
Purposeful Direction	You have clear goals. Your energy is focused on what you can control.

Adaptability	You adapt your behaviour and approach in response to changing circumstances. You see failure as an opportunity to learn and grow from, in order to develop.
Challenge Orientation	You generally do not succumb to pressure. Setbacks don't affect your game or life.

Emotion Regulation	In times of stress, you are able to remain calm and in control of your emotions. You don't worry or get caught up on what others think.
Support Seeking	You can accept support from others when dealing with difficult situations.

Using strategies that were outlined in the previous chapter to overcome negative events can help to develop resilience in you. Adding to these strategies are the ABCs of building resilience:

Adaptability

Accept that challenges are part of life.
We all know things in life change; we move houses, or coaches leave. Change is a necessary element of growth. Without

change, there would be no life at all! However, change can often be daunting for some athletes.

Recent research has found that young people who are more adaptable were more likely to have higher self-esteem and have a more concrete sense of meaning and purpose in life. In the same study, a strong correlation was found between resilience and adaptability. The more you see challenges as opportunities to grow, the more you will grow and become more resilient.

Resilient people have a way of accepting challenges head on and using them as an opportunity to learn. When faced with a negative or challenging situation, they will typically ask what the solution is, or what they have learnt out of it.

This strategy can be used if you are not-so-resilient to develop a learner mindset for these challenging situations. Ask yourself to use learning questions. Typical questions can be "What is useful here?" or "What can I take out of this?"

Using a learning questioning approach rather than the usual blaming approach, such as "I did that wrong," encourages learning and growth.

Build Positivity

Research shows that resilient people display both negative and positive emotions in difficult situations[9]. This means: whilst you may be upset with losses and have to steel yourself through adversity, you will also see the significance of pushing through challenges, and place a positive spin on the outcome.

On the other hand, for those who are not so resilient, and mostly negative; when things are good, they are good; when things are bad, they DON'T COPE. To add to this, due to our evolutionary survival mechanisms, our brains are naturally wired to pay more attention to negatives than positives. However, in reality, we actually experience more positive events in our lives.

To improve your resilience, challenge your reflexive thoughts. Address your self-talk, especially when you say "this never" or "I never get that." Count up your number of successes and failures. How can a couple of successes add up to never?

The ratio of positive to negative self-talk is of importance. It has been suggested that we need a 3-to-1 ratio of positive to negative experiences to build resilience and increase optimism[3]. Turning negative self-talk into positive thinking is relatively simple, but it does take time and practice to create this new habit. Consider using the following two suggestions:

1. Humour

Ensure you are open to humour. When was the last time you smiled during practice? Make an effort to be funny or smile especially during the during hard times. Laughter is a well-known way to reduce stress and pain levels in both the body and mind.

Just make sure you laugh at yourself and not at others. I have a disabled son, Nicholas, who at the age of five started to learn to walk with crutches. He would fall over often, and we couldn't have him crying each time it happened.

As a way of teaching resilience, we employed the method of getting him to laugh each time it happened. What we failed to tell him was that it was okay to laugh when he fell, but not when others fell. One day, we got a call from the school he attended, asking us to meet with the principal.

The principal was appalled by Nicholas laughing at a child who fell over, and felt that we needed to teach him empathy and respect. When I explained to the principal why Nicholas laughed, all was forgiven, but it taught me a lesson I haven't forgotten.

2. Feed on others' Positive Energy

Aligning yourself with positive, supportive people who you can depend on to be optimistic role models, will allow you to be more positive.

There is actually an overwhelming body of evidence that shows strong social connections increase our resilience in the face of injury. After the 9/11 incident in America, Harvard psychologists analyzed the many US intelligence agencies' personnel teams who were working on the fallout of the event. They found that the best teams were those that had people who gave to their other workmates. The right teammate will be one who enjoys helping others, and likes doing so without expecting anything in return.

3. Create Independence

Become autonomous, independent, responsible, empathetic, and altruistic.

You need to learn to answer those pressing questions yourself to solve problems. Independence will go a long way into making great inroads to building resilience. Whenever there is an issue, ask yourself, "What's the solution to that?" Or even, "What is this trying to teach me?" or even, "What can I do to regain control of the situation?" Really, will worrying over failure help fix anything?

Take time to focus on the things that will make it better the next time. Take a long-term view. Did you miss out on an age group title or record? Remember that none of these are the end game.

What are your long-term goals or dreams? Remind yourself that despite the setback, you are not only learning, but in fact, still making progress toward your long-term goal. Even when injured, remember, no one can magically overcome an injury or an illness; but you can look for other opportunities. For a swimmer, a shoulder injury is a great opportunity to work on building up kick strength and endurance. You can control your response, and ensure you follow the necessary treatment or rehabilitation so as not to waste the work you have done so far.

At some stage of our lives, we will all experience failure. Sometimes the simplest way to feel better is to release some of the pent up emotions and stress generated by just doing something else, a bit like changing the channel during a scary movie. We all get to that point in a scary movie when the tension builds and you just can't cope, and what is our natural reaction? Reach for the remote control and change the channel. I am guilty of doing this; it allows my heart to stop pounding out of my chest, so I can keep watching the rest of the movie.

Another way of blowing off steam is to sweat it out. When a race hasn't gone the way it was anticipated, it is best to get back out there and sweat it out. Engaging in exercise helps re-wire the brain to find solutions. It also releases the pent up emotions and allows the body to find the energy to move on. Exercising releases endorphins, which will help you feel better and let go of the negative emotions.

Are you Growing or Fixed?

Coaches and parents only want the best for athletes. Every action, every word they utter sends a message which is interpreted by athletes, but not always in the ways we intended. Society tells parents that they should constantly boost their child's self-esteem. But just like a seedling that is over watered and over-fertilized eventually dies, so too does the opportunities for you as athletes, when you are praised too often or when it really wasn't deserved.

I don't think most parents are aware of the destructive attitude they are creating within you.

Athletes that have been praised too often, for no apparent reason, are those who:

- Aren't the fastest, but certainly think they are. Always wanting to be the leader, or to be in front of everyone else. Sometimes this occurs to the point where the others in the team get annoyed, and soon vent their frustrations with the coach

- When asked to move to the back of the pack, then make an all-out effort to get back up to the front, but after a few minutes can't sustain the pace, and get in everyone's way.
- Interfere with others so they can maintain a higher place, or be in the lead by cutting corners. Or cheat in doing skills correctly just so they can finish first.

If this isn't you, you probably know someone who is.

There are only two types of people in the world: those with a fixed mindset and those with a growth mindset.

These mindsets, have been studied intently by world-renowned Stanford University psychologist Carol Dweck. For over two decades, she has studied in particular, their influence on achievement and success. Her research found that praising, for no apparent reason stops athletes from learning, which means they fail to reach their real potential.

Similarly, it was found that often those with a fixed mindset:

- Reject opportunities to learn if they might make mistakes[10,11]. And when they do make mistakes, rather than fix them, they try to hide those mistakes or blame something else[12].
- They also believed if they were smart then they shouldn't need to put in any effort[13].
- They couldn't handle obstacles, in fact they usually decrease their efforts and consider cheating to stay "smart" or "better"[12].
- They didn't accept or listen to feedback well[12].

Ultimately, we want all athletes to have a growth mindset. With a growth mindset you understand that ability can be developed. You focus on improvement instead of worrying about how good you are. You work hard to learn and get better, without being worried about asking for assistance.

From Dweck's studies we know that improvement can only come by working at tasks. For example, you didn't just wake up and start writing, the more you practiced the better you got. From neuroscience which underlies the growth mindset, we have learnt that the more physical tasks are performed, the more nervous connections to the brain are strengthened. This process makes the brain smarter by 'rewiring' the brain to perform the actions quicker and better. There are plenty of scientific experiments to show how this works.

A growth mindset looks like this:

Belief
You will grow more and succeed with persistence and practice.

Embrace Challenges
Learning may be hard but it can also be fun.

Effort leads to Mastery
Everyone can improve if you work hard enough, somethings just take a little longer than others.

Persist with setbacks
Setbacks only spur you on to try harder and learn more.

Learn from criticism
You listen keenly to criticism, in the hope that you can take away advice which will help you prosper.

Others success inspires you
When others are successful, you feel there is still opportunities for you if you keep working hard.

Compare this to the alternative of a fixed mindset. A fixed mindset is the equivalent of quitting before you start. People with fixed mindsets quit all the time. If they can't immediately succeed, then they feel they are wasting time, and soon stop. They don't think about challenging their learning process or approach to the problem. They see no purpose in working harder, or devoting more time because it amounts to nothing. They can't improve any further, because they believe that talents are already ingrained and pre-determined. People with a fixed mindset are those who tend to start off very successful in life. Initially, everything they attempt comes easy to them. When things become difficult, when they reach high school or a more elite level in sport, they suddenly start to struggle. The following picture highlights the traits of those with a fixed mindset.

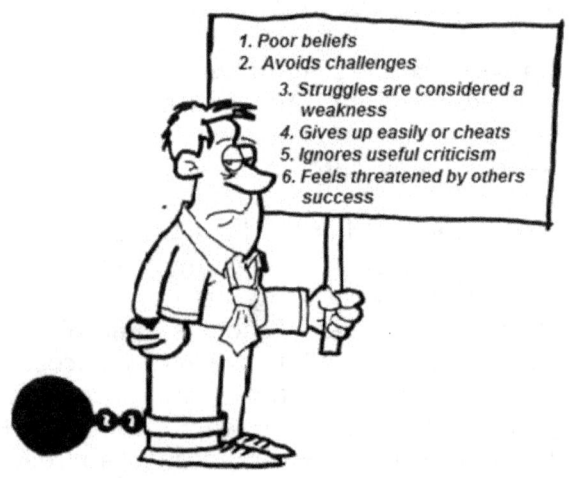

Belief
You are as good as you are ever going to get.

Avoid Challenges
Learning can be both not fun and hard. It may uncover that "I am not really smart after all, so I won't take the risk to be shown up".

Struggles are considered a weakness
If I am good, I shouldn't be struggling. If I have to work at it, it might show that I am really not as talented as I think I am.

Gives up easily or cheating
If it is hard, I can't be good enough. To hold my head high, I can either cheat or stop early with some excuse.

Ignore criticism
If people criticize me, that they must be wrong about what they are seeing. So I can't listen, or I may not be accepting of that advice.

Feel threatened by others success
When others are successful, it suggests that I am not as good as them, and I need to be better.

So to succeed in sport you need a growth mindset, and really, to build a growth mindset is easy if you follow this simple process:

1. Acknowledge and embrace your imperfections. Instead of complaining about having short legs, use it to your advantage. For example, in soccer, short legs are good for quick foot work, the ability to accelerate fast with great agility.

2. Accept challenges as opportunities. Each opportunity develops new learning and possible improvement, be it physical or mental.

3. Try different learning strategies. What works for some doesn't necessarily work for all.

4. Replace the word "failing" with the word "learning." When you make a mistake or fall short of a goal, you haven't failed; you've learned.

5. Being the "SMARTEST", "BEST" or "FASTEST" doesn't work. If your coach and/or parents are using this language readily, get them to read up on growth mindset.

6. Stop seeking approval. You started sport to have fun, you don't need approval now.

7. Value the process over the outcome. I repeat! Have fun and return to the enjoyment of learning

8. Have a purpose. Dweck's research also showed that students with a growth mindset had a greater sense of purpose. Keep the big picture in mind.

9. There is no fast track to speed. Learning fast isn't the same as learning well, and learning well sometimes requires allowing time for mistakes to happen.

10. Accept all criticism as positive. Sometimes people can be harsh, but they only say things with the intent to help. Keep your chin up and listen.

11. Provide regular opportunities for reflection. Take a few minutes each day to reflect on what you have achieved and learnt.

12. Place effort before talent. Talent will get you to the start but effort will take you to the finish.

13. Cultivate grit. Those with that extra bit of determination will be more likely to seek approval from themselves rather than others.

14. Abandon the image. Your best is only the same as everyone else. We all have two arms and two legs, and bleed when cut.

15. No "buts", use the word "yet." Dweck says "not yet" has become one of her favourite phrases. Whenever you are struggling with a task, remember you haven't mastered it yet.

16. Learn from other people's mistakes. While I do have issues with comparison, it is important to realize that humans share the same weaknesses.

17. Goals are important. Make a new goal for every goal accomplished. Growth-minded people know how to constantly create new goals which continually keeps them stimulated.

18. Take ownership over your attitude. Once you develop a growth mindset, own it.

Keeping up with the Kardashians

It is difficult to move forward and allow change to happen if we are "scarcity" focused. A scarcity mindset is one where we believe that everything is limited, and thus it is better to be selfish then generous. Unfortunately, and it may seem ironic but having this mindset, usually results in getting the exact opposite of what want. In the same way, "Keeping up with the Kardashians" and our unending need to compare our abilities, often takes us down that "scarcity" path...usually leaving us frustrated with where we are at, the progress we are making, and where we stand, compared to our competitors. As I have said earlier in this book, comparisons will often cause issues. Comparing can leave us feeling like...we never have enough, look good enough, are skilled enough, tall enough, happy enough, etc. When we spend our time comparing ourselves we never gain or get to a place of fulfillment. And then we end up accepting that "scarcity" mindset...which is the belief that "there's not enough to go around." When we entertain ideas that we lack things such as intelligence, time, money or other resources we need for success, we soon believe that we can't achieve that goal. After all, in most sporting contests, awards are only given to the first three place-getters, from the large numbers who enter.

Unfortunately, many in society have a scarcity mindset, while the happiest people have an abundant mindset. The scarcity mindset is an incredibly toxic mindset to have. So why is this? Well, simply put... when you have a scarcity mindset, you are constantly telling yourself that there is not enough in the world for you to seize. It can be quite painful for the individual and create a lot of unnecessary fear, anxiety and desperation. This attitude usually stems from insecurity: if there's a limited quantity of something good in the world, then why would you ever deserve it. But it also comes from a fear of success.

Far too many talented, hardworking people suffer from a negative view of the world and themselves. They fear success because they believe that they don't deserve it.

To overcome this scarcity mindset, you need to believe in the law of abundance, and in particular, that of opportunity. The law of abundance, is a Universal Law which states that the universe is abundant, always expanding and growing. For you this means understanding that there is limitless opportunity in the world. Anything you can think of, anything you want to do or accomplish is achievable so long as you are willing to put in the effort necessary.

An abundance mindset can help you improve your performance since with it, you experience less pressure and anxieties within your own mind. So how do you achieve an abundant mindset? Very easily, by changing our focus.

Focus on the abundance

What you focus on, you will soon start seeing everywhere in your world. Our brain contains a reticular activating system (RAS), or extra-thalamic control modulatory system, which is a set of connected nuclei responsible for regulating wakefulness and sleep-wake transitions. Due to evolution, our brain is designed to conserve energy. We either focus on:

- Dealing with threats in our environment and learning how to put out fires, or
- Focusing on ways to master our environment and work toward higher order goals that are important to our well-being.

There are so many distractions and demands in our everyday life, that it seems almost impossible to stay focused at times. Our RAS helps make this process of paying attention and being focused a little bit easier. The RAS acts as a filter sorting out what is important, what needs our attention, and leaving what is unimportant to be ignored. When you start focusing on specific opportunities, your RAS will help to focus your mind. You suddenly become aware of things that previously you may not have paid any attention to in the past, but now are useful or important to you and your desire. This will allow you to see the abundance in your world that you may be missing right now. Soon ideas and opportunities to make things happen will start to "pop up" in your world. It's almost a bit freaky how solutions for you will appear.

Now you know how, create abundant opportunities that will help take you to the next level.

As Paulo Coelho says in The Alchemist,

> *"When you want something, all the world conspires in helping you achieve it."*

PART THREE

Self-Confidence

Self-Confidence

"Poor self-confidence is not related to lack of ability"

Anon

Olympic Athletes are some of the best competitors in the world. It often surprises people when I tell them that these athletes have confidence issues just like everyone. For all of us, at some stage of our life we will experience confidence issues, regardless of whether we're elite level performers, final year exam students or in our job every day.

We all question ourselves. **Self-confidence** is the degree of trust or faith that you have in yourself and your abilities.

When you have good self-confidence you often see yourself in a positive, yet realistic way. With good self-confidence, challenges are not so fearful; you have the conviction to be strong, and/or the courage to admit your limits. In sport, self-confidence is often associated with qualities like mental toughness, grit, belief, courage, and heart just to name a few. Words such as these are often said when an athlete is successful. Research has shown that very self-confident athletes have more successful outcomes, whilst those who lack self-confidence have less experience with success[14]. In other words, when you lack self-confidence, you will consistently perform way below your potential.

When your self-confidence is depleted, it is often the "little voices" inside our head that can cause the most damage. For some athletes the damage can be so great it interferes with their enjoyment of the sport, eventually forcing them to dropout.

You may not know it, but the amount of confidence you possess in sport can be measured. (You can do the test yourself, it is in the Free Stuff on my website: http://www.joannelove.com/vealey-s-trait-sport-confidence-inventory-tsci)

Even if you are said to be typically confident by nature, sometimes the circumstances associated with competing mean that "in the moment" our confidences levels can wane badly. For example, David Beckham's attempt at goal when England faced Portugal in the quarter finals of the European Football Championships in June 2004. In the throes of the nail-biting penalty shoot-out, he lost confidence "in that moment" and hoofed the ball over the crossbar.

You are probably wondering by now, what makes us more confident. Well I am glad you asked, in order of importance the nine factors are shown in the picture below[14]:

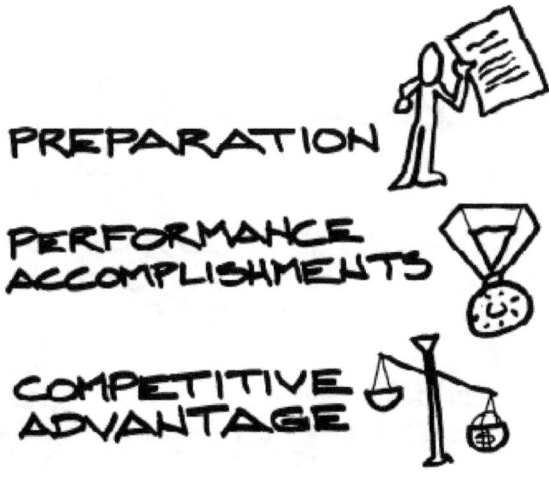

EXPERIENCE

SOCIAL

INNATE FACTORS

COACHING

TRUST

SELF AWARENESS

You will find these symbols throughout the book. Some of these factors we can control whilst others we can't. Now we know what the factors are - let's get started on understanding them. I will show you how they can impact on your confidence levels and teach you some techniques that you can apply to booster and/or control their impact.

Get Ready

There are many ways to prepared for the big day. Before we tackle some of the minor ones, let's deal with the most important one first.

Your competitive routine

Your competitive routine, which is finely tuned over time will not only improve your coping skills, but also allow you to achieve peak performance on game day.

The competitive routine is individual, and the extent of complexity varies between different athletes. Those who easily get an attack of nerves or anxiety will need a more comprehensively developed routine, whilst those who cope better will only need a very light routine.

In developing the competition routine, things that should be considered and implemented at different stages includes, but isn't limited to these:

- Reviews of process goals – what is your mastery.
- Cues and reminders to assist with focus and re-focus when needed.
- A well-rehearsed mental visualization of this performance, following the documented performance plan.
- Being prepared for something out of the ordinary that might impact on this performance, and how you can handle this situation.
- Warm-up routine, and in particular, what elements are of high focus.

At the 2008 Australian Swimming Olympic trials, one of my swimmers, a "**Wannabe**" had a good chance of making the Australian Olympic team in the 400m Individual Medley, however, this swimmer was renowned for being a "choker". In the lead up to the event, John (not his real name) worked with a psychologist on a weekly basis to create and implement a well-developed competition routine in an endeavour to see him perform at his best.

This routine included the walk from the marshalling room to the pool deck, the lane announcements of each swimmer, even how he would wave to the crowd when his name was announced. Nothing was left to chance. Every aspect outlined above was included in this preparation. This routine left him calm and in control.

John swam the race of his career, scoring a massive personal best, but very sadly, missed out on a place on the Olympic team by only a fraction of a second.

John's next swim, the 200 Butterfly, was a totally different story. Unfortunately, the psychologist working with John only prepared him for that one swim. John went into the final of the 200 Butterfly with a strong chance of swimming a personal best, and another opportunity for that elusive place on the team. Prior to the final, John and I sat down and tried to create a routine similar to the one he had established for the 400 Individual Medley. But it was all too late, because the routine wasn't planned and prepared early enough, John didn't have enough time to mentally visualize the tiny details to leave him feeling in control. Because there were holes and things left out, he soon lost control of the situation. The self-doubt took over and in the end he swam a time well over his best.

The moral of the story is not to leave your planning and preparation to the last moment. Be well versed and clear on what you need to do.

Okay, so let's break this down further, and build on each of the points in the competitive routine.

Know your Masterplan

Too much obsession about future results hinders our ability to focus on opportunities. Remember, no matter how hard we try we can't control outcomes. As part of your mental preparation plan, you need to focus on the important components that make up your performance; the processes. Unfortunately, what generally occurs is that those components are often forgotten as you start to focus on the outcomes that are desired from the performance, such as a win or a required time. Establishing a clear methodology to bridge the gap between objectives and outcomes will see you become more in tune with what you need to do. This will stop a lot of negativity that may otherwise be created.

So, on game day, become a master at knowing what processes you need happening to achieve the mastery in your performance. What is your masterplan?

Firstly, you need to differentiate the types of goals. The **Outcome goal**, this is a goal that is totally out of your control. For example: Being the most dominant defensive player on the field.

Then we have the **Performance goals**, which relate to what we are working to achieve, and helps set the direction, keeping us motivated to the task. In the previous example of being the most dominant defensive player you can, this could mean being on your opponent within two seconds of them possessing the ball.

Lastly, there are **Process goals**, which are completely under your control. They are the "baby steps" you take to develop your skills to achieve your performance and outcome goals. Process goals are what you must practice each day in training or on game day. For example, to be able to pick up your man more quickly, you need to improve focus, concentration, and communication to read the ball and your opponents. Process goals are actually a great way to help focus attention. By focusing on process goals you are diverted from thinking about unhelpful things, including those which promote self-doubt. In addition, they allow you to be in control of your performance – which makes you MORE CONFIDENT and less anxious.

The four types of **Process goals** and examples are:

> *Physical* – can be as simple as the warm up, or as complicated as the level of intensity in each stage of a longer race.
> > e.g. 30min pre-determined race warmup routine
>
> *Tactical* – Your race plan – either, what it is or you sticking to it!
> > e.g. Go out easy through first lap, build each lap thereafter
>
> *Technical* –Technical points that will help with your desired level of performance –
> > e.g. maintain stride between hurdles
>
> *Mental* – Your focus, attitude or concentration

e.g. use a pre-event routine before each race to avoid mental distractions

What's your Mantra?

A performance cue is a short statement said to yourself to help refocus concentration, commonly called a mantra.

This statement consists of 2-5 words, and you can use it consistently to regain focus and concentration. Performance cues also help to combat and fight against those negative and distracting thoughts that sometimes rise to the surface when competing.

These statements should be easy to remember, propel you into action, and help maintain focus. To be really effectual they should display your ATTITUDE and BEHAVIOUR and spark ENERGY to keep you on track.

To determine what attitude the statement should contain, ask yourself the following question.

"If I were the best athlete I could be, how would I look and act?" For example: shining, calm, dominating or determined.

Take your time in making it both personal and believable for you. When you achieve this it will then give you the most benefit. To provide the spark of energy it is also important that the statement remains positive.

Examples of Mantra's are:
- Time to shine
- Breathe, believe, and battle
- Keep calm and carry on
- It's not the destination, it's the journey
- Man up
- Steady, ready, poised, winning

To get the most out of your statement in competition takes practice. Ensure you say your mantra at different times and in different stages of practice competitions. Combining the statement with a few centering breaths, will allow you to not only refocus, but also decreases muscle tension caused by any resulting anxiety.

The easy technique to employ is:
1. Inhale a breath through your nose lasting a count of 4. Make sure you breathe deep and feel your stomach move.

2. Hold the breath for 1-2 seconds.

3. Exhale the breath through your mouth lasting a count of 4.

4. While you are exhaling, state your mantra in your mind.
5. REPEAT

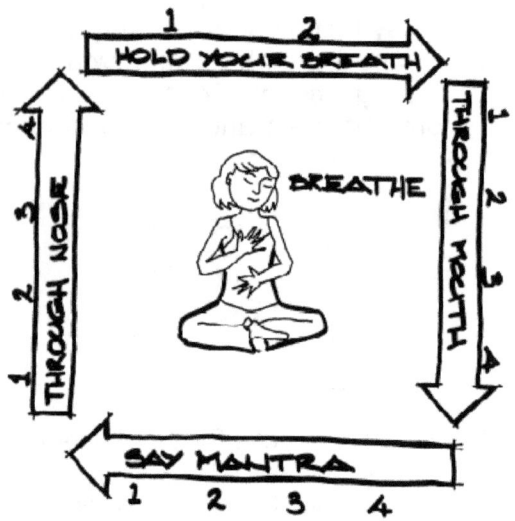

Practicing this technique regularly will see it come to life easily during a major event and in other stressful situations. This will allow your mind to calm and remove those unwanted distractions.

Monkey See, Monkey Do

A well-rehearsed mental visualization of your desired performance, following the documented plan can take your performance to another level.

Visualization is such an underutilized tool to rehearse a positive mental experience and assist in attaining new beliefs. Many of our top athletes, from Muhammad Ali to Michael Phelps, have used visualization to think about such things as technique or winning. Rugby player Jonny Wilkinson was a big believer in using visualization to assist him with putting the ball between the posts. He visualized the ball travelling along its path and took in the sights and sounds of the strike on the ball and the movement of the ball through the air.

Many years ago, I watched a video of a young girl with her eyes closed, tapping a key on a table, a little like the old Morse code tappers. In front of her was a screen, and behind that screen was a projection of her swimming. She couldn't see the projection, but the amazing thing was that her taps were in time to the strokes she was taking.

The video has since vanished, like lots of other things did when the East German wall came down. That swimmer was Kornelia Ender, four-time Olympic gold medalist, who has since been stripped of those medals due to drug use. Whilst we now know that the East Germans used every method they could for their swimmers to win, a big component of their program was visualization.

What we do know is that visualization triggers neural firings in the muscles and helps to create new mental blueprints. One fascinating study using visualization found that muscle strength improved 13%, when athletes only visualized they were practicing bicep curls.

Exciting new research in this field is suggesting that whilst we still need to practice the skills and undertake the required training, the mind can prime you for both improved muscle growth and performance. In addition, it helps you to think clearly about how you will react in different situations before they occur, and in doing so it implements a 'mental warm-up'.

Conquer the What if's

Being prepared for something out of the ordinary that might impact on this performance, and how you can handle this situation, will help build your confidence and shut down any internal talk immediately.

If you are going to a major competition for the first time, in a new venue, try to get some familiarity with it. Anything that helps your familiarity with the situation will reduce the sense of significance that the unknown can create.

Some examples of having plans in place ready for the big day include:

1. **Restless sleep prior to competition**

Many athletes have trouble sleeping before a big event, this is no different than a student the night before exams. Practice competing with little or no sleep at minor meets. Once you know you can perform well in this circumstance, you will not fret so much over the lost sleep and in some instances this knowledge may actually help you to sleep better when it is really needed. Learn meditation to help induce sleep. Don't start learning the day before the meet; meditation takes many months of practice to do well.

2. Competition Arena

The sights and sounds of a competition arena can be the undoing of many athletes. Whilst you may normally be in control at your usual home arena, the atmosphere or size of a different stadium can send some peoples nerves into overdrive.

Participate in a trial meet at the venue where the actual big meet will be held to help you acclimatize to the venue.

If you can't get to the venue prior to the meet, organize to have photos and floorplans of the venue stuck up on walls at training. Talk about the venue as much as possible with your coach and other team members. This will help you feel like you know the venue before you even arrive.

3. **Emotional State required for peak performance.**

The emotional state required for you to perform well is an important aspect of planning. Reflect on your past performances. What were you feeling before you competed well? Not every athlete will be the same. Some might need to be angry to lift and perform well. If you can't get angry by yourself, what do you need to help you get to this state? Similarly, some may need to be left alone, whilst others won't want to be left alone. Determine what works for you, and if necessary ask your coach to help plan your best strategy.

4. **Post-Performance Recovery**

Both wins and losses generate strong emotions. Do you know the best ways to deal with these? A poor performance can send an athlete spiraling out of control.

Endorphins are released in response to pain and stress, and helps to alleviate anxiety and depression. It also diminishes your perception of pain.

So how can you elevate your own Endorphin level? Try Laughter. Even the anticipation and expectation of laugher e.g. attending a comedy show, increases levels of endorphins. Take your sense of humor to the competition with you.

SOCIAL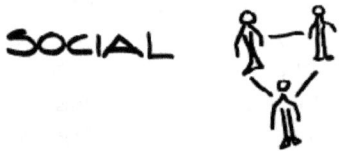

Finding several things to laugh at during the day is a great way to keep your endorphins flowing.

Picking up the Pieces

For some athletes, losing an important game is almost like losing a family member.

Just recently, I overheard a couple of guys on the train talking about a crushing defeat. The first bloke said he 'almost put his fist through the wall' after a loss. What he said really made me stop and think.

"In the 2004 Grand Final, we'd won three on the trot. Port Adelaide came out raging in the third quarter, then it was all over. The siren blew and I cried and I cried.

"It's been a long time between drinks. Now I look at losses as a way to analyze their performance, and work out what the team did right or wrong and where I think they could have done better".

Just like everyone else in this world, you need to know how to handle losses or failures to pick up the pieces and learn from the experience. After all, some of the greatest sportsmen and women have failed many times over before they have won. This book is filled with examples.

You can learn from their big meet losses and eventually move on to bigger and better success by following these four facts:

1. Success isn't a one-way street
When you believe that winning is the only option you are actually more likely to not succeed. When you don't win, the despair you experience is often devastating for you and everyone around you. It is always interesting to watch how different athletes handle losing. Your actions can either help or hinder the process.
You will help the process by:
- **acknowledging your feelings:** "Why are you so upset?", did you perform badly? Or are you upset at losing?

- **Put your feelings into words:**
  For example, are you embarrassed, disappointed or confused? Putting your feelings into words will help increase the recovery process, and you will calm down faster, and this allows you to have the ability to create solutions.

2. Keep Calm and Carry On

Being calm allows you to be more aware of what is happening around you. For example, how many times have you been given some bad news over the phone, to only hang up and not remember a word of what was said? Calmness will allow you to listen and accept. Regardless of the performance, you need to be calm and in control so you can accept the advice that is given to create improvement next time.

3. Listen or watch a repeat

A video replay can reveal all the little faults that caused your issues during your performance. This video can be replayed at a later time, when you are not so emotionally drained.

Listen when others athletes are receiving feedback about a similar fault. When you are not so emotionally invested in the outcome, you will be able to pick up on some of those little details you may have missed.

4. Open your eyes to the blind spots

Learn to think about the things that may have affected the outcome. In the case of a bad swim, it could be physically a poor turn, or mentally you were too focused on winning and not thinking about the process.

A great technique to use to learn and recover from our mistakes is to write the mistake down, and throw it away for good. By throwing the mistake away it will help you let go and think about the positive solution. So get yourself a sheet of paper, and fold it in half.

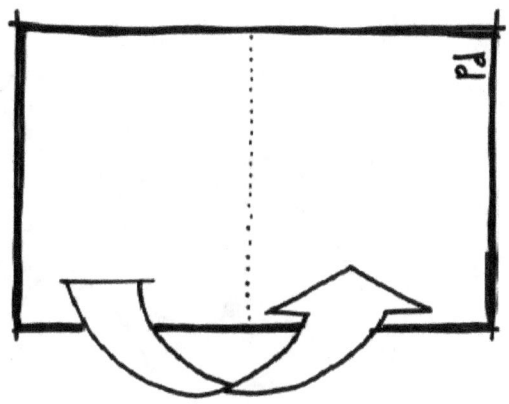

On the top half of the page, write what the skill was and what mistake you made On the bottom half of the page write down the skill again, and this time write down how you should have performed that skill. Now be a superman and rip your page into two.

Throw the top half in the bin, and keep the bottom half somewhere prominent to remind you of the solution, so you don't perform that mistake again.

Sometimes opening your eyes to these errors can sour the performance even more, but in the long run it will stop you from repeating the same mistakes again unintentionally, and ultimately lead to better success in the future.

We all know that losing sucks. But if you work on the above points, it will make you a better competitor in the future.

Create Success

As I have already shown you there are various methods to help build your confidence. One of the most influential sources of confidence is often past successful performances, but how do you go about creating successful results.

Past good performances can create a positive confidence cycle which is highly linked to the technique of "goal setting".

We all know about setting goals, but the majority of athletes still don't do it correctly. What I am not going to do is go through how to do each step correctly, but I am going to highlight the things that you need to do, which could be making the difference for you in achieving your goals.

Firstly, I need to teach you about a chemical that naturally occurs in your body – **Dopamine.**

Dopamine is a naturally occurring hormone which motivates you to take action toward your goals then it gives you a surge of reinforcing pleasure when you achieve them. Hands up - Who has won at a competition, then felt absolutely miserable later that day, or the next day? Well that's the dopamine hangover. Just like sugar gives you a high, the resulting effect after is a low. Of course the higher you go the lower you can be afterwards.

When we don't set goals or your goals aren't strong enough, you will have low levels of DOPAMINE. Low levels have been linked with self-doubt and lack of enthusiasm.

The first investigations of dopamine started with studies of rats. Scientists placed two piles of food out for them. There was a tiny little pile just before a small obstruction, with a large pile behind the obstruction. Those with lower levels of dopamine didn't try, but just took the easy smaller pile of food. Those with higher levels were the go getters, and got the higher pile of food.

If you are low on dopamine you can naturally increase your levels by creating a series of little finish-lines. By regularly achieving these finish-lines, you will release and increase your dopamine levels. But it's crucial to actually celebrate after each achievement. Go out and buy some favourite food, or something new whenever you meet a small goal.

How then do we avoid the dopamine hangover; when you tank out after a massive high?

Your ACTION - Create new goals before achieving your current one. That ensures a consistent pattern for experiencing dopamine.

Now let's look at how you create goals that will really work!

Write it out

Many athletes have goals, but never actually write them down or say them aloud. By writing out your goal you activate the Psycho Neuro Motor Activity, in other words, it enters our subconscious, and allows every learning style to be activated.

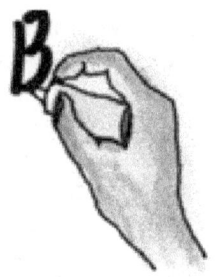

For example, it's:

- **Kinesthetic** - because you write it, and feel it
- **Visual** – view it with our eyes
- **Auditory** – sub-vocalize it with your mouth
- **Auditory-digital** - you plan it out

It is the Sum of all its Parts

It's great to have a goal, but what do you need to make this goal happen. Break your goal down into parts and keep working on it until it's complete.

The more you have your goals broken down into parts, the more finish lines you will create, allowing for your dopamine levels to increase, and help you to have both more self-confidence and direction.

Take a look at the complexity of this goal setting chart.

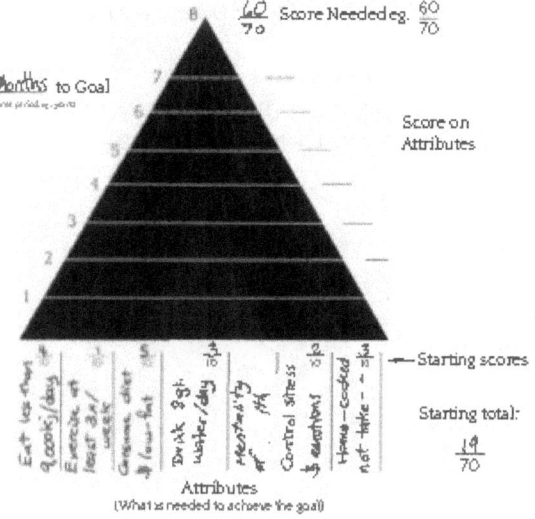

Prioritize
Now that you have lots of little sub-goals from your one big goal, you need to organize the list. What's the sequence, what are the most important goals that must be achieved first, what are the least important. In life there is what is called the 20/80 rule – usually the first 20% of the things you do in the achievement of a goal usually accounts for 80% of the results you get.

The last thing is to make sure you:
Do something every day to achieve it!

Success Breeds Success

Performance accomplishments can be one of your strongest providers of increased sport confidence.

When you play well, or accomplish a skill successfully, you build confidence in both that activity and you are also willing to try something harder. Personal success breeds confidence, while repeated personal failure diminishes it.

The Winners Effect

This effect occurs when the success we achieve creates its own self-reinforcing state of euphoria and generates a positive feedback loop. More success therefore becomes a competitive advantage to an athlete.

COMPETITIVE ADVANTAGE

In other words, if we win, we create greater confidence in ourselves to win again. The winners effect for a long time was considered to just be a myth. However, latest neuroscience research is starting to confirm it really does exist. In addition, statistical analysis is also backing up these results. Researchers rigorously examined a database of 630,000 professional tennis matches and found that the winner of the first set had a 60% chance of winning the second one and, thus winning the match itself. (Michael Phelps's Olympic results would also suggest a similar conclusion.)

Shining in the spotlight

As we can't always be winners from day one, this is a great exercise to promote that effect and hopefully help you in bridging the gap between your ability and confidence:

1. Imagine a huge spotlight beaming down on the floor one metre in front of you, like in a stage show.
2. Think back to one of your great performances, it doesn't need to be a win, just one that made you feel great.

3. Think about what made it a successful outcome and how everything just seemed to flow without much conscious effort.
4. Now look back at you in that performance from a distance. Examine each of your five senses. See yourself inside the circle and excelling. Imagine exactly what the 'you' inside the circle is seeing, hearing, feeling, and smelling. Notice the 'taste of success' in your mouth.
5. Now step into the spotlight and become you in that moment. Again, notice what you are seeing, hearing, feeling, smelling and tasting.
6. Notice exactly what this feels like so that you can reproduce it at will whenever your confidence is waning.

Positive Self-talk

Alternatively, you can build confidence by positive self-talk. Remember Mohammed Ali's "I am the Greatest!".

Transforming thoughts such as
"What if I miss the shot"
into "I will get the next one in"

or "I don't think I am good enough"
into "The coaches think I am good enough to do this".

This is also where your mantra comes in, as we learnt about in a previous chapter.

Exploit others Success

Being involved with successful people can also considerably boost your confidence, especially if you believe that the performer you are involved with is similar to you with the qualities or abilities you both hold. Consequently, you feel: 'if they can do it, I can do it'; or maybe you are actually better.

A good example of success creating success, was shown at the 2004 Athens Olympics when British runner, Kelly Holmes surpassed expectations to win two gold medals in the 800 and 1,500 metres. Shortly, after Holmes's second gold medal, her teammates ran in the 4 x 100-metre relay and they too were ranked as outsiders. Spurred on by her success, the Brits stormed home a fraction of a second ahead of the famous USA quartet to score the Brits their third gold medal. The British relay team believed their extraordinary success was achieved by the mental boost that Holmes' success created.

Just remember we are all created equal, we all have two arms, two legs, and bleed. What can you do better than your opponent? This little piece of knowledge can make a big impact on your self-confidence when next you meet up.

Take a moment to analyze their weaknesses. This person probably has doubts and fears just like you. If you spend time thinking about your opponents, focus upon which weaknesses and frailties you might think you may have in common so you can get a better handle on them. Here are some specific guidelines to help you:

1. Watch them in action. Get some video footage and analyze what most often causes things to go wrong for them. It's possible in certain conditions they don't cope – such as Paula Radcliffe in the heat and humidity of the Athens Olympics. Or psychologically, such as Jana Novotna who was on track to defeat Steffi Graf in the 1993 Wimbledon final. A double fault resulted in one of the most sudden

and heartbreaking collapses Centre Court had ever witnessed. She unfortunately had her eye on the win and not on the play.
2. In an individual sport that requires technical skills such as golf, make a point of congratulating your opponent when they have a lucky stroke but say nothing when they are genuinely skillful.
3. In team sports, look for players who are easily wound-up and find out what triggers it. Italian defender Marco Materazzi used this technique, controversially, in the final of the 2006 Football World Cup. Word is that Materazzi allegedly insulted French captain Zinedine Zidane who reacted badly. Zidane violently head-butted Materazzi and was immediately sent off as a result. Italy went on to win the match;
4. Some opponents will get highly perturbed by what they perceive to be unfair refereeing decisions, usually lashing out. Make a point of being friendly and respectful towards match officials and, in doing so, at a subconscious level at

least, they are more likely to adjudicate in your favour in any close call.
5. When your opponent is having a good run of form, use alternate tactics. American tennis star John McEnroe was the undisputed master of slowing a game down, when his opponent was in a flow; his behaviour earned him the title of 'SuperBrat'!

Be an Ego Master

I think we have all encountered that athlete who has the biggest ego going. As such, their confidence often seems unshakeable. But for some this confidence can go too far, becoming arrogance. Whilst confidence can be your protector, arrogance can be your archenemy. At the elite level in particular, most have built a huge ego. After all, they have achieved great accomplishments to take them to the top, and that couldn't be done without a great mental attitude. However, for them to accept there might be a chink in that armor, that they might need some help dealing with issues, it can seem like they are not tough enough or even a failure.

A most pertinent example is that of James Magnussen. James Magnussen was pre-Olympic favourite for the 100 freestyle, leading the world by nearly half a second. James' cockiness in the lead-up to the London Games was seen by many psychologists as a "red flag" warning. Of course, the rest is history, the missile failed to fire in both his own individual swim and also in the 4 x 100 relay. To this day James' is still trying to restore his confidence and self-belief.

You are probably asking what is the difference between people who feel confidence and those who are arrogant?

Confidence arises when we feel good about ourselves, and we show socially desirable traits such as conscientiousness, and agreeableness. Whilst when we are arrogant of course our ego is in overdrive, and we often show undesirable social traits such as disagreeableness and sometimes aggressiveness. Arrogance is often a result of having low self-esteem or even shame.

Wake up and smell the roses, your arrogance is telling you, that you need help and fast.

Some of the techniques in the earlier chapters may help you, just don't be frightened to use them.

Superstition

Don't mock that player in your team who may always has to wear the red jocks on under his shorts to bring him luck. Even the greatest professional basketball player, Michael Jordan is superstitious. While leading the Chicago Bulls, Jordan wore his University of North Carolina shorts under his uniform in every game because he believed they brought him luck. In fact, it was necessary for him to wear a longer pair of shorts, to cover the second pair underneath.

Sport is full of superstitious athletes, such as those who perform a specific routine before a competition, to those who carry or wear lucky charms. Then there are those athletes who won't do certain activities just because they believe it will bring them bad luck.

Current research has shown that having a lucky token or a ritual can improve your performance by increasing your self-confidence.

You'd be surprised at the number of top athletes who have a tendency to follow superstitious routines, for example, Tiger Woods wears a red shirt on tournament

Sundays, which is often the last and obviously the most important day of golfing tournaments. Have a look at his shirt color the next time you see him play on TV.

Athletes who have rituals or charms, also have a tendency to set higher goals for themselves on competition day than other athletes[15]. These athletes are also aware that these are 'not rational,' but that doesn't stop them using them no matter what level they are.

Do you have a ritual or a lucky charm you use in other areas of your life? Could you make it work for you on Game Day?

PART FOUR

Anxiety

Anxiety

Anxiety is one of your major obstacles when it comes to succeeding in competition. This anxiety may come from fear of injury, or fear of failure, but usually anxiety is related to performance and I commonly hear comments such as "Am I going to be good enough? Can I do what I'm trying to do?" So whether it's a performance timing anxiety in terms of being good enough that day, or an injury, or a fear of failing, or even a fear of success, it all kind of gets lumped under that anxiety category.

With all the different ways anxiety manifests there are also different ways to find solutions to what may be YOUR issue. It comes down to either:

1. Changing your thought patterns and your physical self will follow.

2. Or, changing your physical self and your thought patterns will follow.

Following up on the story about Roger Federer at the start of this book, it took him six years to get on top of things due to his poor mindset. So as it takes time to win these head games, we better get started now.

Melt Down

You are standing in front of the goal posts; the pressure is on. Can you score? Can you control the pressure? You line up the ball, you kick,……..and it goes out on the full. Does that sound like you?

When a player fails to score a goal, others will usually comment on the physical performance. For example, did they time the kick right? If you're watching an AFL game on TV, the camera will show a close up replay of the kicking action, followed by the commentators discussing how he didn't position the ball correctly, or the angle wasn't right.

In all my years watching sports on TV, I have never heard a commentator discuss the possibility that the player's mental state may have impacted on the scoring shot. Just like the commentators here, many spectators, coaches and parents do not understand the complicated connection between the mind and the body.

As a coach, pressure is one area that I am well-acquainted with. Why can some athletes cope really well with major competitions, whilst others who promise so much never deliver the goods when it counts? Pressure affects everyone in various ways; those who succeed have learnt to harness the pressure they feel and use it to their advantage.

So what is pressure? Pressure in sports is the perceived or real expectation that athletes have to perform to a certain level, and if they fail to do so, there will be negative consequences. In reality, there are no negative consequences except for the ones that exist within the athlete's mind.

Pressure can manifest itself in many different forms. For example, being in a competition that is perceived as being important, such as a championships or trials; increased media attention, especially the intensity of media attention during Olympic year; expectations expressed by people that are important to you, such as your coach, teammates or parents; the list could go on and on.

You can use pressure to your advantage, firstly you need to understand why pressure has an impact on us. The mind and the body live in a highly interrelated relationship, in which our actions and responses can cause extreme reactions in either entity. This is very easily summed up in the Feedback Loop.

The Feedback Loop starts when the pressure athletes experience causes a consequential effect in the body. When athletes succumb to pressure, the resulting mindset is one of doubt, reluctance and even a lack of trust in their own ability. Remember, it is the mind which initiates the body's movement and reactions. As such, the negative emotions of doubt, fear, etc., which have been built up in your athletes' minds actually hinder their physical movements, making them rigid, tense or even tentative to take action.

This restriction will make the outcome of the efforts poor and create bad experiences. These bad experience will fuel the pressure when they go to compete again, which in turn further impacts on their behaviour. It is a vicious cycle, as shown over the page.

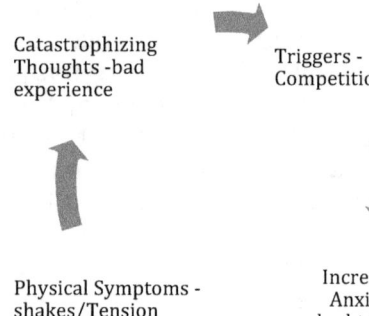

Controlling these emotions, thoughts and feelings will ultimately assist athletes in overcoming these fears and therefore performing better on a more consistent basis.

So how do we break this feedback loop? You need to learn that you have a choice. You have a choice to let the pressure help or hinder you. You have a choice on how you interpret the competition environment. You have a choice to listen and accept what people say to you. In others, you can be a rock and deflect the pressure, or a sponge and let it all seep in.

Here are the techniques to turn pressure on its head, break the loop, and use it to your athlete's advantage:

1. **Learn the facts**

It is important that you can recognize the events that trigger feelings of pressure. When you start to feel the pressure building, you need to consciously stop and take a moment to ask, "What is happening here?"

Learn to answer the questions as an outsider would see the situation. These are the facts! For example, you are at a major meet. What do you see? Maybe this:

Sidney and Georgia are blabbering on about boys. Most of the crowd are reading the program, and some are cheering at the end of a close race.

All of the above are just facts, and none of them are threatening. The more objectively you can assess the situation and control your thoughts, the more they will realise that they are not actually sources of pressure.

2. So what?

The Feedback Loop commences when doubt or fear enters the athletes mind. To help overcome these worries, keep asking those questions repeatedly until their answer has no consequence. For example, if you perform badly – So What? What is the worst that could happen – So What? Keep asking until you have covered every worry you may have and until you can't add anything else which may be bad.

3. Reframe the situation

If you are feeling the pressure build up by sitting in the stands, go for a walk, get outside for a few minutes.

Adrian Moorhouse, 1988 Olympic Champion in the 100 Breaststroke, added enormous pressure to himself by announcing to the world that he was not only the one to beat, but that he also would break the world record at that meet. When the pressure got too great for him, he left the stadium and took a walk outside. Noticing the over- whelming number of cars on the busy freeway, he realised that in perspective his swim was really insignificant to all those people, and probably didn't really mean any- thing to millions of people around the world.

4. Use a mantra

If you are aware of the pressure rising, the use of a mantra (see Part Two) can help counter negative thoughts. Make sure these mantras are part of your competition plans.

5. Focus on the process

As part of your mental preparation plan, you need to focus on the important components that make up your performance; the processes. Unfortunately, these components are often ignored when you start thinking about the outcome you desire. Establishing a clear methodology to bridge the gap between objectives and outcomes will see you become more in tune to what you need to do, and stop a lot of pressure that would otherwise occur.

6. Build familiarity

If you are going to a major competition for the first time, in a new venue, try to get some familiarity with it. As we already outlined earlier in Part two, preparing for your big meet, anything that helps your familiarity with the situation will reduce the sense of significance that the unknown can create. Building familiarity is a simple habit of preparing equally well for each meet and having, as far as possible, the same routine.

Focus

How we focus plays a big part in controlling our anxiety. Successful athletes have the ability to control their focus, by having the expertise to dodge the many distractions that big competition events bring. Unfortunately, for others, the biggest issue with focus is that most really don't understand how it manifests.

Focus is not the ability to concentrate for long periods of time. Many think about focus in the extreme way, believing that you are focused when you are only thinking about one thing, and shutting out all other things. Another misconception, is that many believe that humans find it hard to focus because we are constantly and easily distracted. The latest I am hearing is that Gen Y, (yes that's you), can't focus at all. What a load of hogs' wash!

Just recently, I attended a state-level competition and observed a coach working with a young, very inexperienced athlete. The boy was only in his early teens and was really excited to be swimming in his first final. He was really enjoying the atmosphere. He returned to the stands after his pre-race warmup, calm and relaxed. He was freely conversing with his team mates about what had happened at school as well as the latest Xbox game. He looked like he was in control of the situation, seemingly confident and ready to race well. About half an hour prior to having to attend marshalling, the coach felt that his young charge wasn't sitting quietly and focusing on his upcoming race. In an effort to see him focus solely on what he need to do in the race, the coach removed him from the stands and his friends and took him to a quiet corner of the pool. Observing the situation from a distance, I could see the child's posture and demeanor changing as the coach continued to whisper in his ear. In response the boy was becoming more inhibited and closed with his body position. When he walked out on to the pool deck ready to race, you could see the nervous energy sending shivers throughout his body. As they say, the rest is history. His race was finished before it had even started. The coach, thinking he was doing the right thing in getting his swimmer to focus, was in fact opening the doorway to thoughts that this young competitor was inexperienced at handling.

So what is focus? For athletes, focus is when you are voluntarily able to control your thoughts towards the best execution of the skills that you need in order to achieve successful completion, regardless of distractions that present. That doesn't mean a steely-eyed gaze looking intently toward the finish line, oblivious to all other things happening around you.

Distractions that divert an athletes' attention come from our attention field, which is made up of either internal or external sources.

ATTENTION FIELD

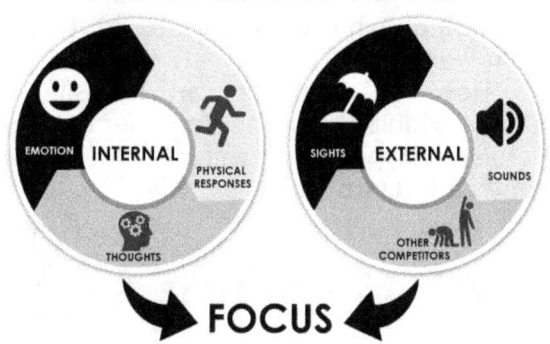

Internal sources of distraction include our thoughts, both negative and positive; our physical responses, for example the nervous shakes; and our emotions. External sources of distraction, can be many things including the size and noise of the crowd and the reputation of competitors.

Focus is about how an athlete goes about controlling all the aspects that present in the attention field. For athletes to achieve prime focus, they often need performance cues, which I talked about earlier.

Where so many athletes get it wrong is that they assume that to be focused, they should be deeply thinking about their future performance. In other words, sitting quietly, not talking to others, and just focusing on what they need to do, to perform well.

However, athletes can actually innately exhibit either an internal or external behaviour type, which will reflect how they cope with distractions.

INNATE FACTORS

Those with an internal focus behaviour will sit and focus on their performance long before the action is due to commence. These athletes need to get into the "zone", and you can easily pick them out by their headphones and their blank, forward-facing stare.

However, internal focused athletes can be easily distracted, so they try to find a place in their minds where they almost go into a trance. This allows them to filter out negative thoughts and external distractions. If you are one of these athletes you can talk about your event in great detail, and are more than ready and willing to listen to instruction.

At the other end of the spectrum are the athletes who exhibit external focus behaviour. If this is you, then you are only switched on when you are about to perform. Should you start to think too early about the race, all hell will break loose!

For you, focusing too soon is like opening a door and letting in every negative thought, criticism or anxious thought. Be careful with the pre-race, don't go into detail. Try to remain light, calm, and even share a joke, with those around you. Allow yourself to be distracted by everything other than information or thoughts about the race. You will benefit by sitting with another team member and sharing some gossip or something that interests you both. This will work to keep your mind off the impending performance.

In many prolonged sporting events, such as tennis matches or football games, it is not unusual for those who exhibit external focus behaviour to start playing well initially, but after a few poor plays, lose control of their thoughts and let distractions take over, beginning a downward spiral in performance.

Here are some techniques to help you learn what your distractions are, and how to deal with them. Some of these techniques can be used for both externally or internally focused athletes. With trial and practice, you may find some methods work better than others. Firstly, you need to know what type of athlete you are!

Know your distractions
Having an inside knowledge of what your distractions are, can help you to control them, instead of them controlling you.

Think about your last performance – when did you feel your nerves get worse, and you started to lose control. Write them down. Was it walking onto the footy field and hearing the roar of the crowd or was it your reaction to seeing your competitor in the ready room. Breakdown your distractions into two columns, one that is external and one that is internal. The footy field reaction would go in the external column, whilst the emotional experience of seeing a competitor goes in the internal column. See below for other examples. Your attentional focus is the opposite of your greater column. For example, if you have a large external distraction column this means you would be more inclined to be an internal focused athlete. As you have already read, these athletes need to control their reactions to the sights and sounds around them. Knowing your distractions will also aid you knowing what techniques will work best.

Music

Music can aid you in two ways; it can pump you up or calm you down. For anxiety, we need the music to calm you down. It can be helpful in small doses or urgent need. This method simply encompasses, putting on some relaxing music, or nature sounds, or even a guided relaxation meditation soundtrack. I am sure you can find what you like on YouTube or iTunes. You can even use this method at home if you are naturally anxious, and it will help to lower your overall anxiety levels.

Some of the following methods can provide alternative solutions. Not all athletes can utilize this method, during or prior to competition due to the physical need for equipment.

5,4,3,2,1 See, Hear, Feel

This is an easy and great method to help externally focused athletes, especially those who often allow the negative voices in their head to win.

As I said it is really easy – you first look for and say either in your head or out loud:
5 things you see, followed by 5 things you hear, and lastly 5 you feel. For example, I see the green grass, the line markings, the goal posts, the other players, the ball on the ground. I hear the birds chirping, the whistle blowing, a child crying, a mother screaming, and a dog barking. I feel my shorts around my waist, my back against the chair, my feet on the ground, and breeze against my hair and my shoulder against the wall. Then you repeat it with 4 things you see, 4 you hear and 4 you feel. Followed by 3 of each, 2 of each and 1 of each. You can either keep repeating this

sequence until you are ready to compete or stop if you have everything in control.

Deep Breathing

Be aware of your breathing, if you're anxious, it will more than likely be that you are only breathing from the top of your chest. Your breathing is likely to be quick and shallow. Try breathing from the top of your chest now. Fell the rush of blood go to your head, no wonder you can't control your anxiety because you are actually adding to it. With deep breathing you will not only learn to breathe properly, but it will also help to relax you. Just so you know, you can't be relaxed and keyed up at the same time. Relaxing and breathing will help cancel out the anxiety. This method works best if you can catch changes in your breathing early before it gets out of control. When your breathing gets out of control, it becomes a little harder for it to return to normal. With one hand on your chest and the other on your belly, take a deep breath in through the nose, ensuring you feel your belly rise not your chest. The goal is to take six to ten breathes per minute for approximately 10mins to gain the benefits of relaxation.

There is also a wonderful app on the market called "Breathe". This app is both instructional and practical, as you also can breathe in time to a controlled breathing pattern, which ensures that you breathe slowly and deeply.

Save it for a rainy day

Save your worries for another time, or even for a rainy day. This is a tactic that helps control anxiety in the long term. I know many athletes who start worrying about the following day's big events when they get into bed at night. It is the perfect time for the "mind gremlins" to take advantage. After all, you will be very relaxed, and all the major events of the day have ceased, so it seizes its opportunity to let loose. This method may sound a little weird at first, but I know many athletes and their coaches (yes coaches) who use it. It works best if you have legitimate concerns about your impending performance, such as, have I planned enough time for warm-up prior to my event. What you do is tell yourself you won't worry about it right now, but you promise to do it at a pre-designated time in the future. For instance, you may tell yourself, it isn't that important right now, so you will think about it over breakfast in the morning. What you are doing is not dismissing your worry, but instead acknowledging it and at the same time satisfying your anxiety. In other words, you're saying, "I hear you. I know it is a real problem, that I do have to deal with, and I will think about it, just not right now."

A similar technique is to write down all the things that are worrying you and put them in a box until you get home. Or in the case of one athlete I know, he leaves them in the glove box of his car when he pulls up for a competition. This is a physical way of telling yourself that you will deal with this but just not today so it doesn't interfere with your performance.

Get Repetitive

It is undisputable that physical exercise is good with helping to reduce our anxiety. Isn't it ironic that the things associated with our sport can cause our anxiety, but physical exercise can and does reduce it. Given this fact, there is also a lesser known method that can also be beneficial, especially for anxiety, which is the use of activities that involve repetition.

By engaging in repetitious diversions we help to create a balance between the mind and the body. None of the activities in the list require much thought or effort. The diversion and repetitive action, allows your mind to get lost in the soothing action. By concentrating on something other than what was causing our anxiety, we soon start to unwind, and any physical tension soon dissipates.

Of course we don't want to wear ourselves out before the big event, so here is a list of a few to try out dependent on your sport:

1. Kick a ball against a wall over and over and over.

2. Hit a tennis ball against a wall, again and again and again.
3. Squeeze and squish clay or Play Doh, oozing it and feeling the sensation.
4. Make a house from cards, blow it down. Repeat. Repeat. Repeat.
5. Jump rope. Count as you jump. When you trip, start over again.
6. Squeeze a stress ball, or any ball for that matter.
7. Color. The purpose isn't the picture; it's the process, the repetitive stroke of the crayon. It is all the rage at the present time.

Another technique is to build familiarity with the pressure by acknowledging it over and over again. "I am going to race in Rio at the Olympics. I am going to race in Rio at the Olympics". Keep repeating until it has no effect on you psychologically. Repetition helps to break down the "emotional charge" that you have placed on the meaning.

For example, many of us, as children, dislike our own names. I hated mine, and always wanted to have a more exotic name. I went through this not once, but twice. When I got married, I agreed to use my husband's surname, Love. You can imagine how I felt every time I used it in my younger days.

Anyway, after many years of using it, now I really don't care. Repeating names or statements over and over again can be locked in and repeated as if in a loop, and after a while they lose their meaning.

One thing to remember is that all athletes have to deal with pressure, and it will exist throughout your careers. How you learn to control this pressure can help you improve your performances when facing high pressure situations.

The Latest and the Greatest

Progressive relaxation, mindfulness and meditation, which all involve very similar techniques might sound a bit wussy, but they are all part of the latest and fastest growing aid to improved athletic performance.

Kobe Bryant is big on meditation along with the rest of his team, the LA Lakers. Meditation involves the skills of learning how to relax quickly and consciously, as well as learning to pay attention to your thoughts. Paying attention allows you to be able to direct your thoughts, switch thoughts, abandon thoughts, and control mental activity at will. Meditation is a great way to learn relaxation and attention at the same time.

Meditation is a skill that takes many hours to master, approximately 100 hours of practice in fact. The best way to learn meditation is by enrolling in a course.

Mindfulness essentially is just a rebranded meditation, but is more related to psychology, and based more on education, scientific research and everyday values and language. There are some differences between the two, one being that meditation must be performed whilst still, whereas mindfulness can be done at any time and we can do it in an instance.

Meditation also focuses inwardly on the body whilst mindfulness is more expansive, and can even be used to attain an ideal state for competitions. Again, there are various courses. There is also a great app on the market called "Headspace", which is a great way to start if you do suffer from anxiety.

Progressive relaxation has been around a long time in the sporting sphere. This practice conditions your body to relax. It is a technique that must be practiced for about 10 mins morning and night, until you can control your body's relaxation process.

The process goes like this:

1. Make sure there are no distractions (ie. phone turned off, do not disturb sign on door, tell others you are meditating so they don't interrupt)
2. Lay down so that you are comfortable.
3. Start with deep breathing. Put one hand on your chest, the other just above the navel

(belly button). Count slowly to two while breathing in through the nose. Your breath should be coming from your belly, not your chest. Meaning, your hand just above the navel should be moving up and down with your breath — not your hand that's on your chest. Count slowly to four while breathing out through your nose.
4. Continue this for about 4 minutes while thinking about how relaxed you feel. Try to let other thoughts drift away. Focus on your breathing and on relaxing, deeper and deeper.
5. Now it's time for the progressive muscle relaxation. Continue the same breathing rhythm. Count to 2 while inhaling, 4 while exhaling. Start at your toes and as you inhale, squeeze the muscles in your toes tight so that they're curled up (squeeze with 60% of maximum strength) . Then, as you exhale, relax your toes while letting go of all the tension

there. Do this tensing and relaxing for each group of muscles, one by one, from your toes to your head:
- Toes.
- Whole feet.
- Calves/Lower leg
- Thigh/Upper leg
- Buttocks
- Stomach
- Etc.

The Finish Line

You've work hard in the months or even years leading up to a major competition, to ensure that you are fully prepared for any eventuality and can perform at your best on competition day. After all, competition is really about maximising short-term performance. Have you integrated routines to enhance your mental skills into the training program? I hope, that after reading this book, you are now able to improve your mindset and boost your confidence skills to promote success in both your athletic careers and later life.

Just remember one size doesn't fit all, so what might work for your friend or your sporting idol, may not necessarily work for you. Be prepared to experiment until you find something that helps you, but also allow time for the effects to occur.

> *What we wish, we readily believe, and what we ourselves think, we imagine others think also.*
>
> *Julius Caesar*

DEFEAT THE COMPETITORS IN YOUR HEAD!

References

[1] Blacher, J. & Baker, B.L. (2002). Behaviour problems and parenting stress in families of three-year-old children with and without developmental delays. American Journal on Mental Retardation, 107, 6, 433-444.

[2] Scheier, M. F., & Carver, C. S. (1985). Optimism, coping, and health: Assessment and implications of generalized outcome expectancies. Health Psychology, 4, 219 –247.

[3] Gordon, R. A., & Kane, J. M. (2002, February). Explanatory style on the soccer field: Optimism and athletic performance. Poster presented at the 3rd annual meeting of the Society for Personality and Social Psychology, Savannah, GA.

[4] Kavassanu, M., & McAuley, E. (1995). Optimism, pessimism, and physical activity involvement. Journal of Sport and Exercise Psychology, 1995, 246-358.

[5] Kauffmann, C., Bonniwell, I. & Silberman, J. (2010). The Positive Psychology Approach to Coaching. In E. Cox, T. Bachkirova & D. A. Clutterbuck (Hrsg.), The Complete Handbook of Coaching (pp. 158-171). London: Sage.

[6] Seligman, M. E. P., Nolen-Hoeksema, S., Thornton, N. & Thornton, K. M. (1990). Explanatory style as a mechanism of disappointing athletic performance. Psychological Science, 1, 143-146.

[7] Chen, L.H., Kee, Y. H., & Tsai, Y. (2008) Relation of Dispositional Optimism with burnout Among Athletes. Perceptual and Motor Skills: 106, Pp. 693-698.

[8] Peterson, C. (2000). The future of optimism. American psychologist, 55(1), 44.

[9] Fredrickson, B. L. (2013). Positive emotions broaden and build. Advances in experimental social psychology, 47, 1-53.

[10] Hong, Y. Y., Chiu, C. Y., Dweck, C. S., Lin, D. M. S., & Wan, W. (1999). Implicit theories, attributions, and coping: A meaning system approach. Journal of Personality and Social psychology, 77(3), 588.

[11] Mueller, C. M., & Dweck, C. S. (1998). Praise for intelligence can undermine children's motivation and performance. Journal of personality and social psychology, 75(1), 33.

[12] Nussbaum, A. D., & Dweck, C. S. (2008). Defensiveness versus remediation: Self-theories and modes of self-esteem mainte- nance. Personality and Social Psychology Bulletin, 34(5), 599- 612.

[13] Blackwell, L. S., Trzesniewski, K. H., & Dweck, C. S. (2007). Im- plicit theories of intelligence predict achievement across an adolescent transition: A longitudinal study and an intervention. Child development, 78(1), 246-263.

[14] Hays, K., Maynard, I., Thomas, O., Bawden, M. (2007). Sources and types of confidence identified by world class sport performers. Journal of Applied Sport Psychology,19, 434-456.

[15] Damisch, L., Stoberock, B., & Mussweiler, T. (2010). Keep your fingers crossed! How superstition improves performance. Psychological Science, 21, 1014–1020.

About the Author

For over 30 years Joanne Love's coaching methods have influenced Australia's leading athletes, coaches, and teams.

"I love to see all athletes perform at their best"

Joanne is a trained psychologist and Leadership Coach. She has also been a leading swim coach for elite athletes for over 30 years. Her unique outlook draws upon years of educational knowledge, her ability to create successful outcomes, and her psychological training, and inspires leaders of all kinds to maximize performance.

To get more information visit:
   www.joannelove.com

www.ingramcontent.com/pod-product-compliance
Lightning Source LLC
LaVergne TN
LVHW051632080426
835511LV00016B/2313